CW01431564

Original title:
Inlaid Pelts Amid the Mermaid Hark

Copyright © 2025 Swan Charm
All rights reserved.

Author: Swan Charm
ISBN HARDBACK: 978-1-80563-277-1
ISBN PAPERBACK: 978-1-80564-798-0

The Dancer's Gaze Beneath the Abyss

Beneath the waves, a secret world flows,
Where shadows dance in the ocean's prose.
The light flickers, a teasing waltz,
In depths where silence weaves its vaults.

Her eyes like stars in the midnight deep,
Whispering tales that the currents keep.
With every twirl, the water sighs,
As mysteries swirl beneath sunlit skies.

Echoes of laughter, both bright and clear,
Dancing with joy, casting out fear.
In the abyss where beauty aligns,
The ocean's heart forever shines.

In currents strong, her spirit wanders,
Seeking realms where enchantment ponders.
Beneath the waves, she finds her grace,
A dancer's gaze in time and space.

Yet as she moves, the shadows blend,
With every stroke, her dreams transcend.
In the depths where the dark things weave,
The dancer knows what hearts believe.

Tapestry of Water and Wind

In twilight's glow, the waters speak,
A tapestry where shadows peek.
Each ripple tells a tale untold,
Of whispers lost in the ocean's fold.

The wind arrives on feathered wings,
Singing songs of forgotten things.
It weaves through waves with gentle grace,
Creating patterns in time and space.

Clouds drift softly, like dreams that swim,
Catching light on a vibrant whim.
The sea's embrace, both wild and free,
Draws together the land and sea.

A brush of mist, a fleeting touch,
Nature's beauty, it gives so much.
With every gust, the canvas sways,
In harmony, water and wind plays.

This wondrous blend of air and tide,
With secrets deep that it must hide.
Together they form a brilliant bind,
In the tapestry of water and wind.

Echoes of the Elusive Tide

The tide whispers secrets on the shore,
Where echoes linger forevermore.
Footprints wash away with the swell,
Leaving behind their silent spell.

A dance of waves beneath the blue,
In each ripple, a dream anew.
The ocean breathes in a gentle sigh,
As memories drift like clouds in the sky.

Moonlight glimmers, a silver thread,
Guiding lost souls where dreams are led.
The elusive tide calls out her name,
A siren's song in twilight's frame.

With each return, the waves embrace,
Carrying hope with tender grace.
In the ebb and flow, fears may reside,
Yet peace is found along the tide.

In the night, where shadows play,
Elusive wonders won't fade away.
They echo softly in hearts that yearn,
For the lessons the tides always return.

Glistening Gems in Seaweed Embrace

Among the stones where the cool waves play,
Glistening gems find their own way.
Nestled soft in seaweed's grasp,
Like whispered secrets, they gently clasp.

Emerald greens and sapphire blues,
Nature's palette, a painter's muse.
In vibrant hues, the ocean beams,
With treasures caught in gentle dreams.

Shells whisper tales from distant lands,
Of adventures written in soft sands.
Each gem a story, each find unique,
In seaweed embrace, the ocean speaks.

As tides recede, the beauty shines,
A chase for light in woven lines.
These glistening jewels, a fleeting chance,
In nature's bounty, they softly dance.

Beneath the sun's warm, golden light,
The sea reveals its falling night.
In the depths where colors blend and grace,
The gems wait still in seaweed's embrace.

Bonds Forged in the Flowing Blue

In the realm where waters twine,
Hearts entwined, a love divine.
Beneath the waves, secrets hide,
Friendship's strength, the ocean's guide.

Tides whisper tales of laughter shared,
When storms arose, we never despaired.
With every swell, our spirits soar,
In azure depths, we yearn for more.

Hand in hand, through currents bold,
The warmth of trust, a sight to behold.
Together we dance in the foamy spray,
Each heartbeat echoes, come what may.

Bright horizons call us near,
Chasing dreams, we conquer fear.
With every wave, our promise stays,
Enduring love, through ebb and sway.

The Arcana of Abyssal Beauty

In shadows deep, where light fades slow,
The sea reveals its artful glow.
Mysteries held in the ocean's breath,
Whispers of life, and tales of death.

Coral castles, treasures rare,
Guarded secrets, hidden lairs.
In the depths, enchantments sing,
Each ripple dances, a fabled king.

Beneath the surface, silence reigns,
In melancholy, deep beauty gains.
The twilight realm, where dreams take flight,
Guides wayward souls to the soft moonlight.

Sea creatures glide, an elegant thread,
Life's tapestry, where stories spread.
Through ancient spells and ocean's blues,
The arcana waits, for those who choose.

Fragments of Color in the Sea's Embrace

Upon the shore, the colors blend,
Nature's brush, a vibrant friend.
Seashell whispers, soft and sweet,
In sand's embrace, where earth and sea meet.

Emerald waves, with golden seams,
Weaving through our cherished dreams.
With every grain, a memory stays,
Captured moments, in sunlight's rays.

A painted sky sings twilight's song,
As flickering stars guide us along.
In every splash, a heartbeat dwells,
The ocean's rhythm, as time compels.

Hearts like petals, drifting free,
Tangled in the briny sea.
With every tide, a story written,
In liquid whispers, love unbidden.

Currents of Long-lost Lore

In the folds of water, tales revive,
Currents carry whispers, alive.
Echoes of sailors, brave and bold,
Stories etched in legends told.

Dancing lights on restless waves,
Ancient songs, the sea's own slaves.
In moonlit nights, the past returns,
With every tide, the spirit yearns.

Forgotten ships with sails now frayed,
In briny depths, their dreams portrayed.
The ocean holds what we cannot see,
An archive vast of history.

Each crest and trough, a memory stirs,
As salt and spray weave through our furs.
In mystic waters, wisdom flows,
Currents of lore, where the heart knows.

Echoes from the Abyssal Floor

Whispers of time in shadows cast,
Among the ruins, memories last.
Voices from depths, they call and sing,
Haunting the dark, the dreams they bring.

Bubbles rise with tales untold,
Secrets of sailors, brave and bold.
Crimson tides with silent tears,
Echoes linger, numbing fears.

In the stillness, truths unfold,
Depths of silence, mysteries old.
Beneath the waves, the stories flow,
A realm where shadows dance and glow.

Ancient mariners lost at sea,
Trace their path in eternity.
Echoing through the ocean's core,
Whispers beckon forevermore.

Dreams Carved from Ocean Currents

Upon the tides, where fancies drift,
Dreams take shape, like oceans shift.
Carried forth on waves of grace,
Floating free in the endless space.

From coral castles, colors bloom,
Crafting visions beneath the gloom.
Whirling in dances, soft and deep,
Secrets guarded, secrets keep.

Beneath a canopy of stars,
Nighttime whispers from afar.
Each wave a brushstroke, vast and wide,
Painting worlds where dreams abide.

In the currents, magic's sway,
Guiding dreams on their gentle way.
The ocean's heart, a canvas bright,
Awakening souls in silver light.

The Language of Hydrated Echoes

In every ripple, a story speaks,
The ocean's breath, where silence seeks.
Hydrated echoes, soft and clear,
Murmurs of worlds both far and near.

Listen closely, let thoughts align,
The sea's own voice, pure and divine.
In every crest, a tale is spun,
As moonlight dances, joining the fun.

Glistening jewels on fluid tides,
Spilling treasures where magic hides.
Each drop a word, each wave a line,
Nature's prose, perfectly divine.

Under the surface, wisdom flows,
The language of tides is all that knows.
In twinkling depths, connection glows,
As the journey of life gently grows.

Canvas of the Ocean's Heart

Behold the canvas, vast and wide,
Where the ocean's emotions reside.
Brushstrokes of blue, whispers of green,
In every hue, a truth unseen.

Waves crash lightly on the shore,
Nature's rhythm, forevermore.
Each splash, a note in symphony,
Crafting dreams from infinity.

Clouds above, like thoughts unfurl,
Mirrored below in the watery swirl.
Reflections dance, alive with art,
Captured finely, the ocean's heart.

Drifting vessels of lost desires,
In the currents, kindled fires.
Weaving tales of those who roam,
The sea's embrace, a welcoming home.

Ephemeral Echoes of Enchanted Depths

In twilight's grasp, the shadows weave,
A tapestry where dreams believe.
In fleeting echoes, hearts align,
The whispers born from ancient pine.

Through secrets wrapped in moonlit mist,
Time dances softly, gently kissed.
Each heartbeat pulses, deep and true,
The magic stirs in shades of blue.

Where laughter lingers on the breeze,
And twilight murmurs ancient pleas.
Beneath the stars, the stories flow,
In echo's echo, magic grows.

With every breath, a lesson learned,
In depths where every candle burned.
A world entwined in fleeting sighs,
Awakening to starry skies.

So linger here where wonders call,
Embrace the shadows, heed their thrall.
For in these depths, the heart will find,
The echoes left by love unlined.

The Art of Submerged Reverie

In silent depths, the dreams take flight,
A canvas drawn by starlit night.
The heart entwined in shadows strong,
A melody like whispered song.

Through veils of time, the visions glide,
In hidden realms, where dreams reside.
With brush in hand, the soul creates,
A world beyond the garden gates.

Each thought a stroke on tempered air,
A masterpiece beyond compare.
Where colors blend in soft embrace,
The art of time, a quiet space.

And when the dawn begins to break,
These reveries, we dare to make.
An echo calls, a siren's wish,
In every moment, magic swish.

So dive into the ocean's heart,
Where each reflection plays its part.
With every breath, a dream we seek,
In artful depths, our hearts will speak.

Shimmering Paths of the Unseen

Through forests deep, where secrets lie,
The shimmering paths invite the shy.
With every step, a mystery blooms,
Amid the light, the shadow looms.

In whispered winds, the stories tell,
Of hidden realms where dreamers dwell.
The moonlight dances on the floor,
A swirling mist, forevermore.

In twilight's arms, the fireflies play,
Guiding lost souls along the way.
Where shimmering paths of stars intersect,
Each heartbeat calls for dreams conferred.

With eyes closed tight, the journey starts,
A symphony of silken hearts.
In every step, the magic sings,
As if the world held wondrous things.

So tread with care, O curious heart,
Through shimmering paths, you're set apart.
Embrace the unseen, let it flow,
In routes of dreams, forever grow.

Tidal Whispers and Artistic Sighs

Where ocean sighs meet silver shores,
The tides reveal what nature pours.
In rhythmic waves, the secrets hide,
Tidal whispers, the world's abide.

With salt-kissed air and sunlit gleam,
The heart immersed in ocean's dream.
Each tide a brush, each wave a stroke,
In nature's lilt, the soul awoke.

The canvas vast, the seas resound,
Through every surge, inspiration found.
In painting skies, in sculpting sand,
Artistic sighs at each command.

As night descends, the stars ignite,
A gallery of endless night.
In every glance, creation swells,
Tidal whispers, the ocean tells.

So find your peace in ocean's sway,
Let art unfold, come what may.
For in the depths, true wonders lie,
In tidal whispers, dreams comply.

Threads of Silk Between the Waves

Beneath the ocean's gentle sways,
Dance silken threads in sunlit rays.
Whispers of tides call forth the deep,
Where secrets of the waters sleep.

Waves weave stories, old and wise,
In the cradle where the sea life lies.
A tapestry of blue and green,
In every shimmer, a world unseen.

The pull of currents, soft embrace,
In watery realms, I find my place.
With every stroke, the ocean sighs,
A lullaby beneath the skies.

Fish dart like dreams, vivid and bright,
Flecked with colors, pure delight.
They trace the threads, with grace they glide,
In this vast world, I shall abide.

So let me wander, free and bold,
Through winding paths where tales are told.
For in the depths, life's magic sways,
In threads of silk, where my heart stays.

Cobalt Dreams in Coral Gardens

In coral gardens, deep and wide,
Cobalt dreams in currents glide.
With every wave, a world awakens,
Where the song of the sea is unshaken.

Beneath the surface, colors bloom,
Life thrives within the ocean's room.
Each coral branch, a tale retold,
Of mysteries watched as ages unfold.

The gentle hum of creatures small,
In perfect harmony, they call.
A dance of life, in azure holds,
A language spoken, yet untold.

Glimmers of light through ripples flow,
In every gesture, a vibrant glow.
As soft as whispers on a breeze,
In gardens where my spirit sees.

These cobalt dreams, they weave and wind,
In nature's cradle, peace we find.
So let me drift in tranquil grace,
In coral gardens, my sacred space.

Shimmering Veils of Aquatic Mystique

In depths where shimmering veils reside,
Mystique unfurls with the ocean's tide.
Aquatic shades in luminous dance,
Reveal the magic with every glance.

Bubbles rise like whispered lore,
Inviting souls to explore more.
With every twinkle, a secret glows,
In the heart of the sea, where wonder flows.

Creatures of grace in playful dive,
In a world where dreams come alive.
From shadows deep to sunlight's kiss,
In every corner, I find my bliss.

With tides that pulse like a beating heart,
In shimmering veils, I play my part.
As currents guide my wandering mind,
I discover treasures of every kind.

Oh, to be lost in this mystique,
In the pulse of the ocean, timeless, unique.
For in these waters, wild and free,
A reflection of my soul is me.

Songs Carved in Pebble and Foam

Along the shore, where waters kiss,
Songs are carved in pebble bliss.
Each wave a note, each grain a rhyme,
In the symphony of space and time.

The gentle rhythm of the sea,
Crafts melodies that set me free.
Like whispered secrets on the sand,
A timeless echo, a guiding hand.

Froth and bubbles, laughter bright,
In this arena of pure delight.
With footprints traced in salty air,
I dance to tunes that linger there.

The sun dips low in a fiery hue,
Reflecting dreams that feel so true.
Each pebble holds a story's sway,
In the ocean's heart, I long to stay.

So weave the songs of foam and stone,
In every wave, I find my home.
For in this orchestra, wild and grand,
I am forever, a part of the sand.

Forests of Sea Grass and Secrets

In the whispering depths, secrets grow,
Where sea grass sways in the ebb and flow.
Ancient tales in the currents weave,
Beneath the waves, what dreams believe.

Mermaids gather as moonlight spills,
In hidden groves, where silence thrills.
Echoes of laughter, a song profound,
In the forest of green, magic is found.

Crabs scuttle by on a sandy path,
While dolphins dance in their joyful bath.
The ocean's heart, a secret safe,
In this verdant world, we find our grace.

Rays of sunlight, a warm embrace,
Flickering shadows, a fleeting trace.
Each rippling tide shares a tale anew,
Of life beneath skies so endless and blue.

So wander deep in the emerald sea,
Where every wave holds a mystery.
In the forests of grass where secrets lie,
The soul of the ocean will ever fly.

Twilight Over the Merfolk's Palace

As twilight drapes the ocean's glow,
And stars awaken, secrets flow.
The palace shines in hues of gold,
Where stories of old in moonlight unfold.

Shells adorn the grandest halls,
The laughter of merfolk fills the walls.
In shimmering gowns, they twirl and sway,
Celebrating night, chasing day away.

With melodies sweet as the sighing sea,
Each note carries dreams, wild and free.
The tide whispers softly to the shore,
In the palace of dreams, we wish for more.

Crimson coral frames their dance,
Every flicker, a sweet romance.
Together they weave a tapestry bright,
Under the watchful eye of the night.

So linger long in this twilight embrace,
Where magic swims in every space.
In the merfolk's realm, the world weaves tight,
A sanctuary under the spell of night.

Harmony in the Deep Blue Veil

In the depths where shadows reside,
Harmony flows like the turning tide.
Each creature sings a note so pure,
In the deep blue veil, they find their cure.

Eels glide past in a graceful line,
While shrimps chant songs in patterns divine.
The ocean's rhythm thrums in the night,
An unseen harmony, a wondrous sight.

With every whisper of the swell,
Secrets of magic softly dwell.
Anemones sway, a rhythm so fair,
In the deep blue veil, we breathe the air.

Octopus paints with colors bright,
In swirling dances that fill the night.
Nature's canvas, a masterpiece bold,
In harmony's grasp, our hearts take hold.

So dive beneath the tranquil waves,
Where voices echo, where the spirit braves.
In the depths of blue, let your heart sail,
To the timeless song of the ocean's veil.

Vibrant Whirls Under Glistening Stars

Beneath the stars in a dance so bright,
Colors swirl in the velvet night.
Each fish leaps, a spark of gold,
In vibrant whirls, endless stories told.

The current twirls in a shimmering flight,
As sea creatures glide in pure delight.
Under the gaze of the moon's soft sigh,
In this watery world, let our spirits fly.

Coral gardens bloom with hues so rare,
A tapestry woven with tender care.
With every ripple, a rhythm plays,
In vibrant whirls, we lose our days.

Join the revelry, embrace the tide,
In this ocean dance, find joy inside.
With laughter echoing through the dark,
Under the stars, we leave our mark.

So twirl and swirl in the ocean's hand,
Where every heartbeat meets the sand.
In vibrant whirls, forever be,
A part of the magic, wild and free.

Rippled Narratives of Myth

In shadows cast by ancient trees,
Whispers of the past dance free.
Legends woven through the night,
Glimmers of truth in the pale moonlight.

Heroes rise and empires fall,
Echoes linger, a haunting call.
Each tale carries the weight of dreams,
Drifting softly on starlit streams.

The phoenix burns, then rises high,
While mermaids sing a lullaby.
A tapestry of fate unspooled,
As time, the weaver, is gently ruled.

With every breath, a story wakes,
Through silent woods and silver lakes.
The past entwines with future's grace,
In mythic realms, we find our place.

So listen close, let tales unfold,
In every heart, a truth retold.
The narratives ripple, wide and vast,
Carrying echoes of the past.

In the Wake of Enchanted Waves

Beneath the surface, secrets lie,
Whispers of magic, a soft sigh.
The ocean churns with stories old,
In salty depths, wonders unfold.

Tides pull tales from long ago,
Where sailors strive through ebb and flow.
Merfolk weave their spells with ease,
While shells conspire on gentle breeze.

A lighthouse stands, a guardian bright,
Guiding hearts through the darkest night.
With every crash of wave on stone,
Life's mysteries are softly shown.

The wind carries laughter, wild and free,
With echoes of dreams wrapped in the sea.
Each grain of sand holds a memory,
Of journeys vast, of eternity.

As dawn breaks o'er a tranquil shore,
Stories linger, yearning for more.
In the wake of waves, we still believe,
In magic's grasp, we dare to dream.

Threads of Mythic Wonder and Woe

In the loom of twilight's glow,
Woven tales of joy and woe.
Every thread a life embraced,
In shadows where our dreams are traced.

The needle whispers secrets sweet,
Crafting fates at time's heartbeat.
Each stitch a wish, each knot a tear,
Suspended moments, fragile, rare.

In the fabric soft, the stories blend,
Warriors rise and lovers mend.
Through ages past, the colors fade,
Yet in our hearts, they are replayed.

With trembling hands, we weave a tale,
Of grandeur lost and hearts unveiled.
The tapestry holds the fire of lore,
A mythic dance forevermore.

And when the last thread pulls away,
We hold the past, come what may.
Through wonder's eyes, the world we see,
In this woven maze of destiny.

Cradled in the Deep Sea's Symphony

In depths where silence sings so sweet,
The ocean's heart, a rhythmic beat.
Creatures twirl in liquid light,
Ballet of dreams beneath the night.

Coral castles rise and sway,
Guardians of secrets, come what may.
Each bubble sparkles, a note of song,
In harmony where all belong.

A shipwreck rests, a tale untold,
Of silken sails and treasures bold.
Whispers echo through the blue,
A melody of hope anew.

The currents weave a story grand,
In every wave, the world can stand.
With time suspended, our hearts unite,
In the deep sea's embrace, pure delight.

And as the stars twinkle above,
The sea sings softly of endless love.
In twilight's glow, let dreams arise,
Cradled in ocean's lullabies.

Whispers of Scales and Silk

In twilight's gentle, fading light,
The whispers weave, a soft delight.
With scales that glimmer, hints of gold,
And secrets wrapped in tales untold.

Among the reeds, the shadows play,
As dreams emerge and drift away.
The silk-thread tides, they hum and sway,
Where echoes of the past hold sway.

When night descends, the stars align,
A shimmering dance, both bold and fine.
In hidden depths, where wonders dwell,
Entwined in magic, bound in spell.

Each ripple carries tales of old,
Of ships that sailed, of treasures bold.
Beneath the waves, they softly sigh,
The moonlit waters, a lullaby.

So listen close, as dreams take flight,
In whispers soft as velvet night.
The silken currents, deep and wide,
Will lead you where the secrets hide.

Tales Beneath the Tides

An olden tale, the ocean sings,
Of mermaids' dreams and lost ship rings.
Beneath the tides, in silence deep,
The treasures of the past still keep.

The waves, they dance with tales of lore,
Of sailors brave who sought the shore.
With each broad swell, a history sways,
In currents strong, the ocean plays.

From coral caves, the stories bloom,
Of shimmering depths, where shadows loom.
In every splash, a voice resounds,
As whispers weave through watery bounds.

Upon the sand, where legends lay,
The footprints fade, then drift away.
Seashells cradle memories dear,
Their echoes ringing crystal clear.

So wander far, where water gleams,
And find the heart of ocean dreams.
For in the depths, the tales reside,
Beneath the tides, where secrets hide.

Echoes of the Ocean's Embrace

The ocean calls in whispers soft,
An ancient voice from realms aloft.
In every wave, a tender song,
Where memories of the deep belong.

With arms of foam, it sweeps the shore,
Embracing hearts, forevermore.
A lullaby of peace it makes,
In tranquil nights, as stillness wakes.

The rocking boats, they gently sway,
In harmony with night and day.
A brush of salt, a kiss of breeze,
The ocean hums through swaying trees.

Look to the horizon, where dreams converge,
The boundary where worlds emerge.
For every crest, a tale retold,
In echoes of the brave and bold.

As twilight falls, the stars ignite,
A shimmering hint of endless night.
The ocean holds a love profound,
In every whisper, magic found.

Barriers of Shimmering Dreams

Across the shore, where dreams unite,
The shimmering waves kiss the night.
In every glimmer, secrets lie,
Beneath the canvas of the sky.

The stars behold, in silent grace,
The dance of tides, a swift embrace.
With every crest, a promise bright,
That dreams can linger, take to flight.

Through misty breath, the past awakes,
Each ripple holds what memory makes.
In whispered tales, the waters weave,
A fabric rich for hearts that believe.

For barriers fade, like morning dew,
When hopes alight on skies of blue.
Let shimmering dreams, like seafoam rise,
And light the path 'neath endless skies.

In every splash, embrace the tide,
Where shimmering dreams and hearts collide.
For in the depths, the magic streams,
A world reborn in whispered dreams.

Secrets Cradled in Seafoam

In the gentle spray of the tide,
Lies a whisper, soft and wide.
Secrets swim 'neath moonlit beams,
Cradled securely in silver dreams.

Waves dance lightly on the shore,
Hiding tales of ancient lore.
Each bubble bursting, a tale untold,
In the embrace of waters bold.

Fishermen speak of whispers deep,
Where shadows of mermaids softly creep.
With nets of hope, they cast their lines,
Hoping to find what all defines.

Ghostly ships in misty nights,
Sing of treasures and lost flights.
While gulls above, with piercing cries,
Watch the secrets ariseth and rise.

In every ripple, a story found,
Of lovers lost and hearts unbound.
A world beneath, enchanting, wide,
Where seafoam cradles dreams inside.

Reflections of a Watery Realm

In a mirror of shimmering blue,
The sky's embrace twinkles anew.
Reflections dance on currents swift,
A watery realm, a timeless gift.

Every drop holds a flicker bright,
Of daydreams woven in soft light.
Beneath the surface, life weaves tales,
Of hidden paths and ethereal trails.

The gentle lapping beckons me near,
To secrets murmured, sweet and clear.
Each wave a canvas of wishes bold,
A tapestry of stories yet untold.

Coral castles rise and fall,
While starfish beneath the surface call.
The dance of tides, a rhythmic song,
Reminding us of where we belong.

Underneath, a world so vast,
Holds the echoes of the past.
In reflections, we find our dreams,
As the water flows and softly gleams.

Patterns of Salt and Silver

Across the shore, the patterns weave,
Salt and silver ask to believe.
With each tide, stories interlace,
Tracing memories from this place.

Footprints linger, washed away,
By the ocean's tender sway.
Whispers of sailors long since gone,
Echo in the light of dawn.

Glistening shells like jewels shine bright,
Tales of the deep in morning light.
Every curve and every line,
Holds a fragment of the divine.

Waves retreat to reveal more grace,
A dance of time in nature's embrace.
Patterns shifting with the tide,
In this kingdom where dreams abide.

Salt-kissed air, oh, how it sings,
Of treasures and of secret things.
In every rhythm, a hidden lore,
Beneath the waves, forevermore.

The Murmurs of Hidden Depths

In the depths where silence speaks,
Lies a world that softly seeks.
Murmurs drift from shadows deep,
Secrets cradled in waters steep.

The shadows curl like whispered sighs,
Where the heart of the ocean lies.
Creatures glide in hushed ballet,
In watery realms where dreams play.

Each bubble rises, a tale unspun,
Of battles lost and victories won.
The deep blue calls with mystic voice,
Inviting wanderers to rejoice.

Where light and darkness softly blend,
In currents that twist, around they bend.
Listen closely to what they say,
For every murmur points the way.

Hidden depths hold the stars of night,
And fragments of the morning light.
In their embrace, the world unfolds,
As the silence reveals, the stories told.

Cascades of Light from Below

In twilight's grasp, the waters gleam,
A dance of hues in silver stream.
The glow of gems, a soft embrace,
Emerald depths, a hidden place.

Beneath the currents, shadows play,
Whispers of night blend with the day.
Crystals shimmer in the tide,
Each pulse, a secret kept inside.

A beckoning of distant dreams,
In every ripple, magic seems.
A lighthouse calls from far away,
Guiding souls who yearn to stay.

With every wave, a story swirls,
Of ancient realms and forgotten pearls.
Life surges forth, a wondrous sight,
In cascades of shimmering light.

A journey ends where it begins,
Submerged in depths where silence wins.
The world above fades out of view,
As light reveals what's pure and true.

Secrets Locked in Aquamarine

In aquamarine, the echoes hide,
Secrets of oceans, deep and wide.
With every wave that laps my feet,
Mysteries sway in time's heartbeat.

A treasure chest lies lost in dreams,
Where light reflects in shimmering beams.
The water's edge, a sacred space,
A threshold to another place.

The whispers swirl like autumn leaves,
Unraveling tales the sea conceives.
In hidden coves, the past remains,
A dance of joy, a thread of pains.

Each salty breeze, a lover's sigh,
As memories drift and softly die.
Beneath the waves, the truth awaits,
In aquamarine, we find our fates.

A mirror to the heart's desire,
Reflecting hope, igniting fire.
As tides recede, we hear the call,
Of secrets locked, yet known to all.

The Weave of Waves and Wishes

In the briny depths where dreams arise,
Waves carry wishes beneath vast skies.
With every swell, a heartbeat roams,
Across the sands where memory foams.

Tangled threads in ocean's loom,
Weaving stories amidst the gloom.
A gentle pulse, a songbird's tune,
Resonates beneath the moon.

Each crest reveals a glimmered thought,
By currents strong, our hopes are caught.
Wishing stones in twilight's breath,
Sing of life and love and death.

The salty breeze, a soft caress,
Carrying whispers of happiness.
In every wave, a promise made,
Of dreams embraced, of fears allayed.

As we drift forth on this blue sea,
The weave of wishes sets us free.
With every tide that ebbs and flows,
Our hearts entwined in ocean's prose.

Fables Born from Brine

From briny depths, the fables flow,
Tales of sailors lost in woe.
Each whispering wave, a secret taught,
In ocean's arms, the stories caught.

The sea's embrace, both fierce and kind,
Burdens shed, and peace we find.
With every splash, a legend spins,
Of mermaids' songs and ancient sins.

Beneath the surf, old dreams revive,
In shimmering light, the past's alive.
A serenade in moonlit shrouds,
Where every wish the ocean crowds.

By starlit paths, the brave embark,
Adventurers chase the timeless spark.
In brine, we drink the tales of yore,
Endless journeys to explore.

The tides of fate dance in the night,
Guiding souls towards the light.
In every grain of sand, a sign,
A story whispers, born from brine.

Harmonies within the Ocean's Lullaby

Beneath the waves, where shadows play,
A melody hums, soft and gray.
Each ripple sings a tale so old,
In whispers of salt and secrets told.

The moon her guardian, casts a beam,
Upon the waters, like a dream.
Starfish twirl in jeweled dance,
While currents weave their timeless trance.

A dolphin's laugh pierces the night,
A haunting song, pure delight.
With every splash, a heart takes flight,
Lost in the ocean's deep twilight.

Shells clatter softly on sandy shores,
Like nature's drummers, keeping scores.
The tide recedes, a gentle sigh,
In harmony, the world goes by.

So close your eyes and listen near,
The ocean's voice, a spell sincere.
In every wave, a story waits,
The lullaby of ancient fates.

The Craft of Celestial Waters

In skies where dreams weave threads of light,
The waters craft a wondrous sight.
Crystals twinkle, a cosmic plume,
Under the stars, in stardust bloom.

The tides are sculptors, shaping fate,
With every crash, they resonate.
Fish dart like whispers, swift and bright,
Filling the sea with pure delight.

Beyond the waves, where wonders gleam,
The craft of water spins a dream.
A tapestry of liquid grace,
In each droplet, a secret space.

The whirlpools twist, a dance profound,
As coral gardens thrive unbound.
With flicks of fins, they carve their art,
Creating worlds that never part.

So let the oceans guide your way,
To where the stars in waters play.
In every splash, a song is sung,
The craft of celestial waters sprung.

Veils of Form and Feathery Whisper

Veils of mist embrace the sea,
Where dreams drift soft, wild and free.
Like gossamer threads of a fairy's sigh,
They dance on air, and not ask why.

The ocean breathes a gentle breeze,
With feathers brushed by emerald trees.
Each whisper carries tales of old,
Of sirens' calls and treasures bold.

Waves curl like scrolls of ancient lore,
Secrets hidden on the ocean floor.
A shiver of scales, a flash, a glint,
In depths unknown, where wonders hint.

With every rise and fall of tide,
The sea reflects both joy and pride.
In feathered whispers, the truth unfurls,
A symphony sung beneath the swirls.

So tread the edge where water meets sand,
Feel the magic beneath your hand.
In veils of form, let your spirit soar,
To the rhythm of the ocean's roar.

The Alchemy of Seashell Muse

In twilight's glow, where seashells lie,
An alchemist weaves, no need to try.
With every grain of sand, a tale,
Of journeys taken, winds that sail.

The ocean's breath forms echoes sweet,
In clinking shells beneath our feet.
A symphony of past and now,
In every curve, a timeless vow.

As waves retreat, they leave behind,
Treasures touched by the world's kind.
Each seashell whispers secrets shared,
Of fleeting moments, hearts laid bare.

Beneath the moon, they shimmer bright,
As constellations in the night.
Nature's canvas waits for you,
With every shell, a dream anew.

So gather 'round, in wonder muse,
In the alchemy of seashell hues.
Craft your story, let it flow,
Embrace the magic the sea will show.

The Deep's Secret Symphony

In shadows deep, where whispers dwell,
A harmony sung, no words can tell.
The ocean's sigh, a lullaby sweet,
Calling the dreams, on waves they meet.

With every tide, a story unfolds,
Of lost loves, and treasures, and futures untold.
The sirens call, with a haunting refrain,
Echoes of joy, mingled with pain.

Beneath the foam, the secrets reside,
In currents swift, where mysteries glide.
The deep's embrace, a velvet gloom,
In its quiet depths, hopes still bloom.

Fins flash like stars, in the night's embrace,
Guiding the sailors to a familiar place.
In the watery cradle, dreams never cease,
As the deep sings softly, granting them peace.

Folklore Woven in Salt and Sand

Upon the shore, where legends lay,
The whispers of ancients beckon to play.
With salt in the air, stories are spun,
Of tides that shape, and battles won.

Shells speak of love, and hearts lost too,
Each grain of sand, a tale to construe.
The whispers of wind carry myths of the sea,
Woven with threads of destiny.

Dancers of dusk, in twilight's embrace,
Weave patterns of life in the soft sandy lace.
Fables of old, come alive on the breeze,
As the waves cradle secrets, like jewels in trees.

From fishermen's cries to sirens' delight,
The echoes of folklore dance through the night.
In the salt and sand, our past intertwines,
With each crashing wave, the heart defines.

Mosaics of Life Among the Waves

In shards of color, the ocean reflects,
The myriad lives, each moment connects.
A tapestry woven from foam and light,
In the depths of the blue, life takes flight.

With every swell, a fresh canvas drawn,
The artist of nature weaves dusk into dawn.
Creatures collide in a ballet so grand,
Each fin, each tail, a part of the plan.

Seashells scatter thoughts of the day,
Echoes of laughter, in salt they play.
Mosaics of life, crafted anew,
Winking at sailors and dreams that ensue.

Currents that pulse with stories abound,
Where time flows slow, and magic surrounds.
In this boundless expanse, let spirits roam,
Among the waves, we find our home.

Lore of the Depths Beneath the Light

In the cryptic depths, where shadows loom,
Lie tales entombed, in the ocean's gloom.
Beneath the stars that shimmer and shine,
The moonlit water conceals the divine.

Ancient whispers ride the rippling tide,
Of mariners lost, and secrets they hide.
In the heart of the sea, where darkness sings,
A treasure of lore, the ocean brings.

Coral gardens bloom like dreams unchained,
Among the bright colors, life is sustained.
The tales of the deep, in silence compose,
The mysteries treasured, that not all can pose.

Fables of giants, in silver waves drift,
Stories spun softly, like an ethereal gift.
In the depths, we find more than what's seen,
For in whispered lore, the soul can glean.

Mosaics of Waves and Whimsy

In the twilight's gentle embrace,
Whispers of laughter dance in the tides,
Each wave a tale, a spark of grace,
As moonlit paths where imagination guides.

Shells shimmer bright with stories untold,
Their colors vibrant, a wondrous array,
Nature's mosaic in hues bold,
A treasure of whimsy where dreams play.

Seagulls glide in a symphonic flight,
Their shadows painting the shimmering sand,
With every swoop, they ignite delight,
Crafting a world where magic does stand.

The sea sings softly its rhythmic song,
A melody woven from depths afar,
Echoes of joy where all hearts belong,
Guiding lost souls to their radiant star.

Mosaics emerge as dusk deepens down,
With laughter and light tangled in the foam,
Every crest a whimsical crown,
Inviting the dreamers to find their home.

The Flow of Dreams Through Tidal Glass

In the realm where oceans gleam,
Dreams flow like whispers through the night,
Captured in a tide's gentle stream,
Reflecting the stars that dance in flight.

Tidal glass frames the universe wide,
Each ripple a canvas of untold tales,
Crafting a world where hopes can abide,
And hearts set sail on the wind's soft gales.

Beneath the waves, secrets softly sway,
Where colors of life harmoniously blend,
The flow of dreams in a magical play,
As time unwinds and horizons extend.

With each glimmer, a wish starts to rise,
Floating like feathers upon the breeze,
A gateway to wonders within the skies,
A journey of hearts where moments seize.

In this dance of the tides, we seek and find,
The essence of life in each golden drop,
For in the depths, our spirits are aligned,
And dreams, like the ocean, never stop.

Hues of a Forgotten Seascape

Beneath the horizon, colors still sigh,
Hues of a seascape lost in the mist,
Where shadows of memories flicker and fly,
And the whispers of what was cling to the tryst.

Coral castles in vibrant decay,
Shell-stitched secrets wrapped in the tide,
Every grain of sand has a story to say,
In echoes of laughter, joy, and pride.

A lighthouse stands with its beacon of grace,
Guarding the shore with watchful delight,
While the waves weave a delicate lace,
Cradling dreams in their glowing light.

The gulls call out in a haunting refrain,
Mournful yet sweet, a lullaby's note,
Reminders of love and the lingering pain,
That dances like sea foam on waves that float.

Yet within this canvas of forgotten lore,
A heartbeat lies, vibrant and true,
For every seascape holds so much more,
Than the hues of a past that fades from view.

Fins Dancing Amidst Enchantment

In the depths where the mermaids dream,
Fins twist and twirl in a magical dance,
Amidst the glow of a silver beam,
They weave through currents, lost in a trance.

The water sparkles with laughter and cheer,
As fish parade in gowns made of light,
Each flip a whisper, enchanting and clear,
A ballet performed in the deep and the bright.

Coral reefs bloom like gardens below,
Homes to the sprites of the swirling seas,
As bubbles of wonder silently flow,
Creating a realm where the heart finds ease.

Through kelp forests, they gracefully glide,
With echoes of magic that linger and swell,
In this underwater realm of pride,
Where tales of adventure and friendship dwell.

So let us dream of the fins that soar,
In currents of joy beneath the waves,
For in the ocean's enchanting lore,
Dancing together, our spirit braves.

Shrouded Whispers in Bracken

In the thicket where shadows play,
Wild secrets dance, then gently sway.
A hush of leaves, a soft request,
Nature's breath in hidden nest.

Glimmers of light between the fronds,
Echoes of laughter, the fae's sweet bonds.
Moonlit paths where dreams reside,
In bracken's arms, the world wide.

Gentle murmurs from the earth,
Songs of sorrow, tales of mirth.
The night unfolds its velvet cloak,
In whispered dreams, the faeries spoke.

Where the owls hoot, and shadows roam,
The heart feels light, the place feels home.
In the stillness, magic stirs,
Among the leaves, the spirit purrs.

In this grove of emerald grace,
Every moment, a soft embrace.
With every sigh, a curtain drawn,
And dawn awakens, night's song gone.

Currents of Melancholy and Magic

Deep in the river, secrets flow,
Whispers of currents, soft and slow.
Over stones that cradle dreams,
Rippling under the silver beams.

A chill that dips in twilight's wear,
Memories haunt the midnight air.
With every wave that rolls and breaks,
A tale is spun, as silence aches.

The moon reflects on waters deep,
Cradled by night, the shadows seep.
An echo of laughter, a fleeting glance,
In the dance of waves, lost in trance.

Glimmers of stars, like wishes tossed,
In melancholic hues, all is lost.
Yet magic lingers in every tide,
Where love once bloomed, but now must hide.

As dawn approaches, the currents sigh,
Revealing truths as moments fly.
In the stillness, solace found,
In every wave, life's echoes sound.

Hidden Realms of Fin and Light

Beneath the surface, worlds collide,
Where fish and fables gently glide.
In shimmering depths, a realm untold,
Treasures of heart, both warm and cold.

Fins that flicker, scales that gleam,
In twilight waters, a silent dream.
Secrets whispered in rippling waves,
Among the currents, the magic braves.

Dance of the minnows, swift and bright,
In ballets formed by pale moonlight.
Echoes of laughter from depths below,
Where dreams in silence quietly flow.

The realms breathe life with every dart,
A tapestry woven, a work of art.
Hidden from eyes that search too wide,
In every drop, a new world hides.

Dive deep, and find the shimmering prize,
In finned realms where the heart truly flies.
In the kaleidoscope, the soul ignites,
Awakening worlds of dreams and lights.

The Allure of Ethereal Waters

Beside the stream, a soft allure,
Reflecting dreams, both dark and pure.
With every ripple, stories spark,
Caught in the glow, the night's bright cloak.

The call of water, enticing, clear,
Whispers of peace, yet laced with fear.
A melody dances through the air,
In the gentle current, spirit's dare.

Starlit creations atop the glass,
Where shadows and light gracefully pass.
Secrets flutter like petals blown,
In darkened corners, the magic's grown.

Each drop reflects a fleeting wish,
An ethereal touch, a lover's kiss.
Where dreams cascade in hush and gleam,
The heart finds solace in the stream.

With arms open wide, the waters call,
A promise of wonders, an echo's thrall.
To wander along the water's side,
Is to dance with fate, in love reside.

Crystals Clinging to Forgotten Waters

A glimmer rests where shadows play,
Among the reeds, in whispered sway.
Secluded pools, with ripples shy,
Reflecting dreams as days drift by.

Moonlit beams on water dance,
Their silvered touch, a fleeting chance.
With every drop that breaks the calm,
A shimmered world, a whispered balm.

Petals drift, on currents twirled,
In quiet depths, a hidden world.
Lost treasures hide in silken threads,
Crystals glowing where silence spreads.

Echoes linger, tales untold,
In emerald depths, both rare and bold.
Wonders spark in depths unseen,
Crystals clinging, soft and keen.

So pause awhile, let waters flow,
And seek the truths the currents know.
In every crystal, every gleam,
Lies history's half-forgotten dream.

A Dance of Fins and Fables

Beneath the waves, a symphony,
Of scales that shine in harmony.
With every flick, a tale unfolds,
In watery realms where magic holds.

The dolphins leap, a joyous flight,
Their laughter echoing through the night.
In coral halls, where colors burst,
The dance of fins, a thirst for thirst.

Bright jellyfish, like lanterns glow,
Waltzing softly, to and fro.
Each ripple tells a story sweet,
In caverns cool, where currents meet.

Anemones sway, with gentle grace,
Embracing secrets in their space.
A dance of fables, old and new,
In shadows cast, a vibrant hue.

As tides pull back, and waters weave,
The ocean sighs, a tale reprieve.
In every splash, a woven thread,
A dance of fins, where dreams are fed.

The Palette of Aquatic Wonders

A canvas stretched where waters flow,
In hues of azure, deep and low.
Coral reefs, like vivid dreams,
Paint life beneath with vibrant schemes.

The fish, like brushstrokes, dart and glide,
In tranquil depths, where secrets hide.
With every wave, a whisper flows,
A palette rich, where beauty grows.

The seaweed dances, in the tides,
A graceful sway, where magic hides.
In shades of green, and golds that gleam,
A wondrous world, a painter's dream.

Beneath the sun, a playful glow,
Reflecting tales of long ago.
The ocean sighs, a story spun,
In colors bright, and golden sun.

So lose yourself in this vibrant sea,
Where every shade sets the spirit free.
In the depths where wonders dwell,
The palette speaks, enchanted spell.

Surfaces That Hold Ancient Stories

Upon the waves, where whispers cling,
Lies history wrapped in ocean's swing.
Each splashing sound, a tale once shared,
On surfaces where time has fared.

Weathered stones, and salt-kissed shells,
Guard secrets of where magic dwells.
Beneath the surface, life has thrived,
In shadows deep, where dreams survived.

The tides unveil, with gentle ease,
A chorus sung by ancient seas.
In every crest, a story spins,
Of loss and love, of souls within.

The echoes call from deep below,
With voices soft, like winds that blow.
They weave like lace, through currents old,
On surfaces that time has told.

So take a breath, and dive profound,
Where ancient hearts and waves abound.
In every splash, in every sigh,
The ocean's tales forever lie.

Whispers of Seashell Secrets

Upon the shore where secrets dwell,
A symphony of whispers swell.
Each grain of sand a tale to tell,
Beneath the waves, a magic spell.

The seashells hold the ocean's dreams,
In shimmering hues, they catch the beams.
They speak of journeys, ancient streams,
Of hidden worlds, where starlight gleams.

With every tide, the past returns,
In fluttered breaths, the ocean yearns.
A dance of life where water churns,
And from its depths, a passion burns.

Listen close when midnight sighs,
The softest song, a lullaby.
With each caress of ocean ties,
The secret world beneath it lies.

So wander forth along the shore,
Let whispers guide you evermore.
In every shell, a chance to soar,
To find the dreams that tide restores.

Tidal Echoes in Luminous Shadows

In twilight's glow, the waters dance,
With shadows cast in nature's trance.
A tidal pull, a fleeting chance,
To join the night in sweet romance.

The moonlight plays on ocean's crest,
An echoing heart in nature's chest.
Where whispers swirl, the waves attest,
To every dream, both bold and blessed.

In luminous hues, the sea unfolds,
Tales of magic from long ago.
As silver glimmers in waves so bold,
Life's cherished secrets in tides flow.

With every ebb, the waters flow,
In currents deep, the stars aglow.
A dance of light where shadows grow,
Tidal echoes, a night's tableau.

So stand beneath the sky's embrace,
And let the tides your heart replace.
For in the waves, love finds its space,
In luminous shadows, we find grace.

Enchantment of the Moonlit Tides

Enchanted shores, where dreams collide,
The moonlit tides, a mystic guide.
Each wave that crashes, pure and wide,
Awakens hearts with gentle pride.

Soft whispers curl in salty air,
A serenade to night so rare.
With every tide, a lover's prayer,
To cradle hopes, beyond compare.

In silvery pools, reflections gleam,
A world of wishes, night's soft dream.
Where nightingales in chorus theme,
To celebrate the moonlit stream.

Amidst the tides, the stars ignite,
In harmony, they paint the night.
A canvas woven with delight,
The ocean sways, in purest light.

So linger 'neath the twilight's spell,
Where time stands still, and dreams repel.
In moonlit tides, all hearts can dwell,
Enchantment's embrace, a soft farewell.

Siren's Lament in Crystal Depths

In depths of blue, the sirens weep,
Their haunting songs, the ocean's keep.
With crystal echoes, secrets seep,
Beneath the waves, where shadows creep.

A melody of love and loss,
In watery realms, they bear the cross.
For every heart that dared to toss,
A fleeting glance, a whispered gloss.

Through swirling currents, they lament,
The stories of each soul they sent.
Their voices rise, a sweet lament,
For hearts in pain, their time well spent.

With every surge, the tide rolls back,
A tragic tale in ocean's track.
In crystal depths, the sirens hack,
To weave their sorrow, shades of black.

So heed their song beneath the waves,
For every heart the ocean saves.
In siren's wail, the spirit braves,
A dance of love, the sea's embraces.

Below the Surface

In waters deep where secrets lie,
A world unfolds with a whispered sigh.
Creatures dancing in the muted light,
In depths unseen, they take their flight.

Coral castles, bright and bold,
Stories of ages, silently told.
Currents weaving through the blue,
Binding the ancient with the new.

Echoes of laughter, soft and clear,
The murmur of dreams that linger near.
Bubbles glisten like stars at night,
A realm untouched by day's harsh light.

Anemone sways, a gentle embrace,
Life's rhythm flows in this tranquil space.
Where shadows play and whirlpools spin,
Below the surface, life doth begin.

Yet time drifts on, a fleeting guest,
In silent depths, the heart finds rest.
Emerging tales in each gentle wave,
Below the surface, so much to save.

Above the Stars

In the velvet night, dreams take flight,
Whispers of hope shine ever bright.
Galaxies twirl in the cosmic dance,
Infinite wonders, a timeless romance.

Comets blaze trails through darkened skies,
Drawing forth wishes, soft as sighs.
A tapestry woven by fate's own hand,
Stars beckon gently, a glimmering band.

Constellations sing of stories old,
Of heroes, of lovers, of fortunes told.
Navigators' guides on ships of wonder,
Above the stars, they roam and plunder.

Moonbeams cascade like a silken thread,
Kissing the earth where dreams are spread.
In every heart, a universe lies,
Waiting to awaken beneath the skies.

So look up high, let your spirit soar,
For above the stars, there's always more.
Celestial realms, forever aglow,
Whispers of magic, for us to know.

Heartbeats Beneath the Garden of Waves

In a garden where the waters roam,
Heartbeats echo, finding home.
Waves caress with a soothing touch,
Cradling dreams that matter much.

Barnacles cling to what was once grand,
Stories crafted by nature's hand.
Each splash a promise, each swirl a grace,
Heartbeats whisper, finding their place.

Seashells whisper secrets of time,
Singing riddles in rhythm and rhyme.
Beneath the surface, vibrates the sound,
Of life and magic, entwined, profound.

Dancers twirl in the water's embrace,
In this garden, they find their space.
From the depths where light softly fades,
Heartbeats linger in silvery shades.

So dive beneath, let the current guide,
Where heartbeats pulse with the oceanwide.
Beneath the waves, life's treasures lie,
In the garden of waves, we learn to fly.

Fragile Feathers of Aquatic Grace

In the shimmer of waves, feathers fall,
Fragile and light, they answer the call.
Dancing on currents, a soft ballet,
Wild dreams woven in salt and spray.

Fish weave through the delicate lace,
Each movement a whisper of timeless grace.
With every flick, a story unfurls,
In a world where magic gently swirls.

Kelp sways gently, a lover's embrace,
Lifting the weight of time and space.
Beneath the surface, life's essence glows,
In fragile feathers, the ocean knows.

Bright colors flash, like a painter's touch,
Creating a canvas that sings so much.
In harmony, all beings partake,
Fragile feathers in the dance of fate.

So let your heart drift on currents sweet,
Embracing the rhythm, feeling complete.
For within the water's gentle trace,
Lie fragile feathers of aquatic grace.

Shadows Cast by the Luminous Tide

When moonlight spills on the ocean's crest,
Shadows dance, in quiet rest.
The tide ebbs and flows, a painter's hand,
Crafting stories across the sand.

Underneath the shimmering glow,
Life's secret wonders ebb and flow.
Whispers of magic, woven in night,
Shadows cast by the luminous light.

Seashells gather secrets untold,
In the embrace of the ocean's fold.
Each ripple creates a tale anew,
In the shadows where dreams pass through.

Nighttime's symphony sings so sweet,
With every wave, life's heart will beat.
Tales of journeys through darkness and tide,
Shadows cast by the moonlit glide.

So as you walk by the silver shore,
Listen for whispers, forevermore.
Within the shadows, let your heart abide,
In the warmth of the luminous tide.

Lapidary Treasures from the Abyss

In caverns deep where shadows creep,
Glint of gems in silence weeps.
Whispers of ages echo clear,
Treasures found, yet none drawn near.

With emeralds bright and sapphires bold,
Tales of old in colors told.
Carved by time, each shard a story,
Beneath the weight of ancient glory.

Secrets held in a jeweled maze,
Glimmers dance in the smoky haze.
Legends breathe in the sapphire light,
Crafted fine by the hands of night.

A quest begins, the heart ablaze,
For the brave who dare the darkened ways.
To seek the stones that birth the dawn,
In deep, forgotten realms they're drawn.

But beware the depths where echoes quail,
For treasures sought may weave a tale.
Of loss and gain, each path entwined,
In shadows where the light's confined.

Mosaic of Secrets and Siren's Grail

In twilight's grasp where whispers dwell,
Each piece a note, a nested spell.
Crafted in shades of dreams and fears,
A tale unfolds throughout the years.

With every shard, a legend spun,
Mosaic bright as day is done.
Sirens call from the shores of fate,
To seek the grail and not be late.

Footsteps echo on cobbled stones,
Hearts entwined, chasing the tones.
A dance of fate on shimmering waves,
For every seeker, a path that saves.

The artistry of time laid bare,
A tapestry woven with utmost care.
Siren's song in the evening tide,
Leads the lost to the dreams inside.

From dusk till dawn, the quest will sway,
A journey cast in night and day.
Mosaic of secrets, the heart's great call,
For the brave shall rise, and the brave may fall.

The Glow of Crystalline Waters

In shimmering depths, reflections gleam,
Waters whisper of a thousand dreams.
Each ripple dances, a fleeting light,
A mirror of worlds that hide from sight.

Beneath the surface, secrets flow,
In crystalline glow, a tale to grow.
The essence of life in every stream,
Casting shadows where echoes scream.

With every drop, a story's spun,
Of hearts entwined, of battles won.
The stillness speaks of tales untold,
Of ancient bonds and treasures bold.

In twilight's grasp where wonders dwell,
Each droplet holds a whispered spell.
To drink from these waters, pure and true,
Is to glimpse the magic hidden from view.

So linger long by the glistening edge,
A moment held, a sacred pledge.
For in the glow, the mind can soar,
To realms unknown, forevermore.

A Song of Spheres in Drenched Harmony

In the depths of night, the spheres align,
Whispers blend in a rhythm divine.
Each note a thread in the cosmic seam,
A symphony woven from starlit beam.

From distant worlds, their echoes sway,
Drenched in melody, both night and day.
The harmony sings of time and space,
Uniting hearts in this sacred place.

As raindrops fall on barren lands,
They carry hope in gentle strands.
While shadows dance in the moonlit light,
The spheres unite, dispelling night.

Chords resound as the cosmos spins,
A timeless song where silence begins.
In every breath, in every sound,
A tapestry of dreams is found.

Together we rise, hand in hand,
Guided by tunes from a timeless band.
A song of spheres in drenched harmony,
Echoing truths that set us free.

Beneath the Shimmering Veil

Beneath the shimmering veil at night,
Stars whisper secrets, soft and light.
Moonbeams dance on the silken tide,
Where dreams await, and hopes abide.

Waves cradle stories of old and new,
With every echo, a world in view.
Winds carry tales of lost delight,
As shadows waltz in the pale moonlight.

Beneath the surface, whispers weave,
A tapestry of what we believe.
The depths contain a gentle grace,
Where time stands still in this enchanted space.

In twilight's glow, the stars ignite,
Guiding the lost through endless night.
With every shimmer, a path unfolds,
To realms of wonder, with treasures untold.

So linger here, beneath the sky,
Where dreams take flight, and spirits fly.
In this sacred place, so pure and bright,
We find our hearts entwined in light.

Textures of Twilight by the Sea

Textures of twilight, soft and deep,
Embroidered shadows where secrets sleep.
The horizon blushes in hues untamed,
While the ocean sings, forever unnamed.

Glistening sands like powdered gold,
Breathe life into stories yet to be told.
Rippling waters, serene and wide,
Cradle the whispers of the turning tide.

Stars begin their nightly parade,
Glistening jewels in an indigo glade.
Each wave a note in a symphony grand,
As twilight wraps the world in its hand.

The winds weave murmurs, tales of old,
Of mariners brave and treasures bold.
In this moment, hearts intertwine,
Awash in the beauty, divine and fine.

So linger at dusk, let time stand still,
Beneath the play of the moon's soft thrill.
With the sea as a canvas, we dream and sigh,
For in twilight's embrace, we learn to fly.

Melodies of the Submerged

Melodies linger in waves of blue,
Songs of the ocean, ancient and true.
Echoes of creatures that glide and roam,
Whispers of sailors who found their home.

Bubbles rise, like laughter in play,
As currents spin tales of night and day.
Fins brush past with a delicate grace,
In this hidden world, time leaves no trace.

A shipwreck's ghost speaks through coral and sand,
Of journeys taken, and dreams unplanned.
The beauty submerged, a wonder to see,
In the heart of the deep, we wander free.

Swaying kelp dances to songs of the tide,
In this watery realm where secrets reside.
Every shimmer tells of treasures concealed,
Melodies whispered, forever revealed.

Join the chorus of the deep and wide,
Where the spirits of water and magic abide.
In this serenade, lost souls find peace,
Melodies of the submerged, a sweet release.

Shades of the Sea Serpent's Sorrow

In depths where shadows fold and creep,
Lies a serpent's sorrow, dark and deep.
With emerald scales that gleam like night,
He weaves through the currents, shunning the light.

Once a guardian of treasures rare,
Now he wanders in pain and despair.
Glimmers of lost love haunt his gaze,
In the silence of water, he endlessly plays.

His heart, a vast ocean, heavy with time,
Yearning for freedom, a chance to climb.
Yet shadows linger, and sorrows stay,
In the twilight's embrace, he quietly sways.

Each wave's gentle touch a reminder of fate,
The laughter of children, now bittersweet weight.
He coils in the depths, where secrets don't sleep,
Brimming with sorrows too heavy to keep.

But there in the dark, a spark remains,
A flicker of hope beneath ocean's chains.
In shades of remembrance, he'll rise once more,
For every lost love, there's a chance to restore.

www.ingramcontent.com/pod-product-compliance
Ingram Content Group UK Ltd.
Pitfield, Milton Keynes, MK11 3LW, UK
UKHW022007200125
4187UKWH00037B/928

9 781805 647980